CW00410740

Portrait of the East Neuk

Lorn Macintyre & Peter Adamson

Alvie Publications, St Andrews

First published in the United Kingdom in 2008 by Alvie Publications,
52 Buchanan Gardens, St Andrews, Fife KY16 9LX Tel: 01334 475227

Designed by Jon Gill - *www.gilagraphics.co.uk*

Printed and bound in China by Imago

ISBN:978-0-9511800-5-1

cknowledgements

First and foremost, grateful thanks for the Foreword to Professor Christopher Smout, F.R.S.E., F.B.A., F.S.A.(Scot), CBE., Historiographer Royal in Scotland, founder of the Institute for Environmental History at the University of St Andrews. Thanks also to: Dawn White, photographer, for her professional advice; Sarah O'Connor of Imago publishing for her care and expertise; Gary Adamson for reading the proofs. Thanks to the following for information, advice, amendments, and patience: Tom Hall; Andrew Sherriff; Sarah Mills; Crail Pottery; Anne Morris; Iain Duncan, Rector of the Waid Academy, and his courteous staff; the Head Teachers and helpful staff of St Monans, Crail, Kingsbarns, and Elie primary schools; David Corstorphine; Dr Peter Maxwell-Stuart of St Andrews University; staff at Scotland's Secret Bunker; Jennifer Gordon, Scottish Fisheries Museum; Roger Grundy, Anstruther Lifeboat Station; Tabatha Lamont, Scottish Natural Heritage; Richard Philip, Elie Cricket Club; Liz Anne Fenton, the Guizards; Elizabeth Dickson, Anstruther Operatic Society; David Smith; Dr John Amson and Dr Christine Crow; Mrs Rachel Hart, Muniments Archivist, Department of Special Collections, University of St Andrews Library; Stacey Hoy, The National Trust for Scotland; Dr Joanne E. Taylor; Sue Bradman, Crail Museum; Mary Macintyre. Quotations on the East Neuk of Fife in the 19th and 20th centuries by kind permission of the Scotsman. The material comes from its excellent online archive of the newspaper from 1817 to 1950 accessed through scotsman.com on the Web.

Profit from the sale of this book will be donated to Save the Children.

Foreword

One autumn day in 1981, after I had been appointed to the chair of Scottish History at the University of St Andrews and still had not chosen where to live, I went bird-watching to Fife Ness. The gorse was alive with flycatchers and warblers, and seabirds streamed past the point – it was all so exciting that I decided to rent a house as near to the Ness as possible. There was nothing available in Crail, so I drove a little further to Anstruther, and in the lawyer's window there were particulars of a cottage opposite the Dreel Inn. Thus I became an indweller in the Royal Burgh of Wester Anstruther. Many happy evenings in the Dreel followed. Soon I learned a lot, saw a lot, and found that there was no place in the world where I would rather live.

The East Neuk is the scenery – the wonderful all-pervading presence of the sea, the colours of the coast, the smell of the seaweed and the corn. It is the buildings – the cool and self-contained farms, the step-gabled town houses with their dated marriage stones, the steeples of the burgh kirks high enough to make a statement but not so high as to invite the ever-blowing winds to topple them. Especially the East Neuk is its people – scornful of pretension, gifted with kindness and talent. Centuries of delving and voyaging have given them a horizon as wide as the sky.

This book is a testament to the qualities of the scenery, the houses and above all the people, illustrated by the magnificent photographs of Peter Adamson and described by the lively prose of Lorn Macintyre. It simply encapsulates the East Neuk.

Professor Christopher Smout

The residents of the Bass Rock are known by the scientific name *Marus Barsanus*, after their place of habitation. They are not a tribe of humans, but gannets. These wonderful seabirds were first mentioned in a document sent to the Vatican Council in Rome, outlining a dispute between the owners of the Bass Rock and the Cistercian nuns at North Berwick. The nuns were concerned that the tithe they received on each barrel of fat produced from the slaughtered birds at the autumn cull was under threat. But the Bass Rock colony, the largest on the east coast of Britain, is protected by law and holds approximately ten per cent of the world population of North Atlantic gannets. The Bass Rock remains in the ownership of Sir Hew Hamilton-Dalrymple.

Introduction

'A Fringe of Gold on a beggar's mantle' was how James VI described the East Neuk of Fife. Surely he meant a more opulent and subtle cloak, covering witchcraft, smuggling, religious zeal, treachery, bravery – all the vices and virtues of a unique area compressed into a corner of Fife. This is a lively place. It has a tune named after it; poems written about it by former bards and modern masters like John Burnside and Robert Crawford; and its lore has been recorded by contemporary prose writers like Christopher Rush. Anstruther Easter born William Tennant celebrated the joy and ribaldry of the East Neuk in his epic poem *Anster Fair*.

These are the rich echoes from history, but there is the modern reality. Mechanisation has transformed the East Neuk. The farmer sitting on his horse-drawn harvester has been succeeded by descendants in ear-muffs in glass boxes high above the crop being processed by the huge combine, a search-light on its roof for nocturnal work to beat the weather. Fields have been turned into golf courses, and there is a problem with parking the tens of thousands of vehicles that pour into the East Neuk every season to visit the coastal towns. Everyone seems prosperous, but young people can no longer afford homes in the places their antecedents worked in as fishermen and farm labourers.

These social inequalities can be solved by more affordable housing. Let us celebrate the fact that life is easier now for East Neuk men and women, and that many of them have retained their dialect and their strong sense of identity. The 'beggar's mantle' has become a smart coat.

And such a turbulence of gen'ral mirth
Rises from Anster loan upon the sky,
That from his throne Jove starts, and down on earth,
Looks, wond'ring what may be the jollity;
He roots his eye on shores of Forthan firth,
And smerks, as knowing well the market nigh,
And bids his gods and goddesses look down,
To mark the rage of joy that maddens Anster town.

Anster Fair by William Tennant (1784-1848)

The East Neuk

'Tis a soft west wind, and no mist is in the air,
And the herring-boats go sailing, sailing, sailing far away,
Sailing fast and free
To the mighty open sea,
To the wide and golden east that lies shining over there.

On the fresh green links for a space we'll sit and rest,
While the boats shoot from the pier-head and go sailing far away;
Loud their brave men cheer,
Watching homesteads dear
And kirk and harbour-bar slide back, and faces loved the best.

At the red gabled roofs from our height we can look down,
While beyond with silver track the boats go sailing far away;
Now only women bide
To mind the fireside,
And only children's voices ring within the quiet town.

'Mong seaweed-spread fields the bare--foot lassies hoe,
While the herring-boats go sailing, sailing, sailing far away,
Through firth and northern seas,
T'ward Orkney and Hebrides—
God bless the hardy fishers who o'er stormy waters go!

Lady Anne Lindsay (Barnard) (1750-1825)

Dunino

Dunino Den is one of the most mysterious places in the East Neuk of Fife. For some, it is a place of pilgrimage; for others, a site that disturbs the emotions. You descend by a path fringed with wildflowers which change with the seasons and arrive on a promontory which gives you a panorama of the Den, through which the Kinaldy Burn flows. At your feet you see a hollowed-out pool, about a metre across and half a metre deep. There is also the shape of a footprint in a rock, and an incised cross. Many people who come to this sequestered Den and leave objects in crevices are convinced that is a place of ancient energies which renew you as you stand, hearing in the distance the constant sound of traffic.

A gazetteer of 1857 gives us the lie of the land as it was in the days when men rose in bothies to eat brose before lashing on their leggings and going out to fetch the horses. 'The parish of Dunino is bounded on the north by Cameron and St Andrews, on the east by St Andrews and Kingsbarns, on the south by Kingsbarns and Crail and on the west by Carnbee and Cameron. The lands of Kingsmuir belong to this parish although claimed by Crail. The parish is 3 miles from east to west and 2.5 miles in breadth. With an area of 3315 acres, 2955 are under cultivation, 300 are wooded and 60 are waste land. The highest elevation, Dunino Law from which the parish probably derives its name, is about 300 feet above sea level. It is watered by 3 rivulets that unite into the Kenly or Pitmilly Burn, which empties itself into the German Ocean.'

Nowadays Dunino is a place on either side of the road on the way to Anstruther. But turn off and take the track to the early 19th church and former manse, one of the most charming glebes in Scotland, especially in spring, when daffodils cover the slopes. East Neuk folk continue to be buried in the comforting shade of the church.

Kingsbarns

At harvest time around Kingsbarns, as the golden dust drifts towards the village, one is reminded that its poetic name comes from the fact that grain was stored here before being transported to the royal castle at Crail and the Palace at Falkland. An agricultural community, nevertheless its inhabitants looked to the sea half a mile away as another method of transporting goods, and also supplementing their diet. 'It is a thriving little place, and carries on a considerable manufacture of linens for the Dundee market. The largest and best flag-stones in the country are obtained near the village, and marble of a fine quality is met with occasionally,' a 19th century gazetteer recorded.

In 1810 the Earl of Kellie had a pier constructed to shelter vessels to ship grain and potatoes as far away as London, and to bring in coal and tiles. In 1861-3 a local farmer extended the existing pier and built another to create a harbour, its stones placed vertically to stop the sea lifting them out and flinging them back on the land, because this is a coast of exceptional storms. There are still stones of the harbour in place at Cambo Bay. The farm labourers whose services were bought at the feeing markets of Fife are ghosts walking streets where the houses in which some of them lodged are among the most desirable – and pricey - in Scotland.

In the summer, instead of the fiery arc of a harvesting scythe being swung, it is a golf club on manicured pasture. The name Station Road survives, but the last train on the single track line linking Crail and St Andrews departed in 1965. Kingsbarns is a restful attractive place to live in, and also to rest in, as a tombstone in the churchyard records gratefully:

Through Boreas's blast and Neptune's waves

Have tossed me to and fro,

In spite of both, by God's decree,

I'm anchored here below.

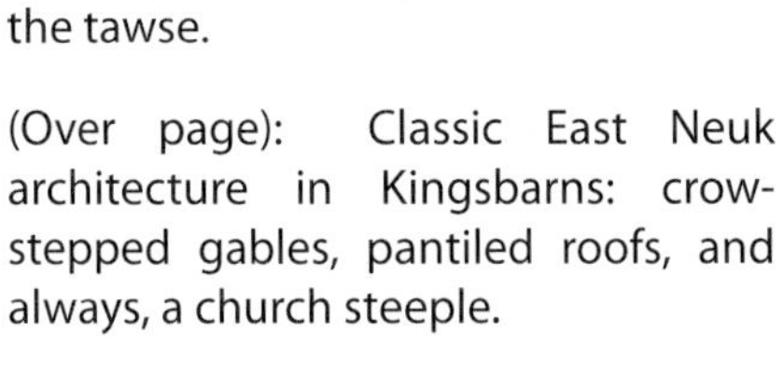

(Opposite): Children skip round a game in the playground of Kingsbarns Primary School, built in 1822 and said to be the oldest primary school in Fife. Computers click where pupils once bent over slates, in the days before school dinners and central heating, when you got as close as possible to the coal fire to dry out after a soaking, and kept as far away as possible from the tawse.

(Over page): Classic East Neuk architecture in Kingsbarns: crow-stepped gables, pantiled roofs, and always, a church steeple.

Bill and Mary Swan warm themselves in their house in Kingsbarns, built by his mother's family in 1898. Bill, a retired banker and skilled amateur radio enthusiast, recalls: 'My father's family came from the Borders. My grandfather built himself a house in Kingsbarns. I think he came here because he was a clerk of works with Sir Robert Lorimer, the architect, who had Kellie Castle. My mother's father kept a boat at Kingsbarns. He made his living from setting lobster creels. He also worked with horses, and used to walk them to Perth, probably to sell them. I was born in Kingsbarns in 1917, an only child. There was no electricity then; we had Aladdin lamps, which we still use when there are power cuts. There were two blacksmiths in the village, and the farm developments you see now were the steadings of working farms. There has been a lot of new building, but a lot of the old buildings have gone, even in my time.' Mary, originally from Kirkcaldy, remembers: 'I taught in the primary school in Kingsbarns from 1936, when I qualified as a teacher. I had lodgings in the village. Mr Wilkie was the headmaster. There were three teachers. Oh yes, the children were well behaved.'

'Mere words cannot convey just how extraordinary the place is. It must be seen to be believed and once seen, it will never be forgotten.' Sir Michael Bonallack, winner of five British Amateur titles and a former Captain of the Royal & Ancient, eulogized over Kingsbarns Golf Course, 7,133 championship yards by the North Sea, where the wind can play havoc with the most promising drives. Designed by Kyle Phillips and Mark Parsinen and opened for general play in the summer of 2000, the course is laid out on land on which golf was played as far back as 1793.

Destruction of Cambo House, Fifeshire, by fire

YESTERDAY morning the fine old mansion, Cambo House, in Fifeshire, the seat of Sir Thomas Erskine, Bart, was totally destroyed by fire. Sir Thomas, Lady Erskine, and family have been residing in London since the 26th April, the only occupants of the house being three domestic servants. Cotton, the coachman, whose duty it was to inspect the house each night, states that about eleven o'clock on Sunday evening he made his usual rounds and found all right, but he was alarmed about two o'clock in the morning by the servants, and on reaching the house he found the lower and middle flat enveloped in flames. Shortly before the alarm was given, the servants became aware of a crackling noise as if falling glass, which they fancied might be some one attempting to enter the house. They ran downstairs to the housekeeper's room, and found it filled with smoke, whereupon they made their exit as speedily as possible, taking time to save nothing of their own belongings. The groom was immediately despatched to St Andrews — about eight miles from Cambo — for the fire-engine. On his road he alarmed the inhabitants of Kingsbarns, who turned out and rendered their utmost assistance. From St Andrews the fire engine was expeditiously despatched, and the Fire Engine Committee of the Town Council, consisting of Bailie McGregor, Dean of Guild Hall, and Councillors Davison and Laverock hastened off to render their assistance. The progress of the flames had, however, been so rapid that ere the engine reached Cambo, which it did about four o'clock, the building was almost completely destroyed. As indicating the intensity of the heat, it may be mentioned that the lawn for about 30 feet from the house was scorched and blackened. Attempts to save any of the valuables were almost futile. The coachman tried to enter the front hall, but the smoke choked him, and he had great difficulty in escaping. Everything of any value was destroyed, inclusive of the family portraits. The only paintings that were saved were a fine portrait of King James II and another of Cardinal Erskine.

The Scotsman, Tuesday, 9th July 1878.

(Opposite): It is claimed that, on that night in July 1878 when Cambo House went up in flames, instead of manning the fire buckets, the East Neuk fishermen were saving the wine cellar for their own consumption, and were overcome by spirits, not smoke, before dawn showed the destruction. But Sir Thomas Erskine was not long in having the rubble carted away and commissioning Wardrop & Reid to build him a fine new mansion. In his book on Fife in the Buildings of Scotland series the architectural historian John Gifford described new Cambo as a 'huge-scale suburbanish villa of the faintly Italianate Georgian-survival type…' Approaching the mansion on a spring afternoon, one delights in the profusion of snowdrops among the trees, wondering how many pairs of hands helped in the massive planting, though snowdrops, like daffodils, wander by themselves. You can buy them to plant in your own garden, or have the bulbs sent to a friend pining for a little piece of the East Neuk. And you can also rent an apartment in Cambo House.

Cambo pig to visitor: 'Have you anything in your pocket for myself and the young one?'

On the road from Kingsbarns to Crail, this silhouette testifies to prime farming stock.

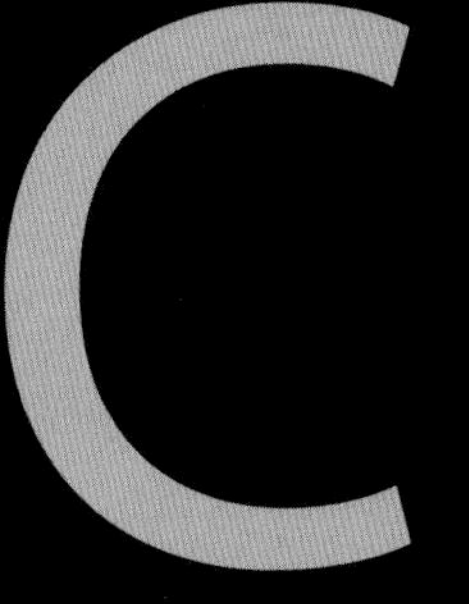

rail

There is nothing brazenly modern about Crail. Some seaside resorts are of yesterday or the day before. They have, as it were, no ancestry. Crail can count back through a long lineage to the middle of the ninth century-long before seaside resorts were thought of. The most easterly town of Fife holds up its head undisturbed by modern ways. It has most certainly a flavour of the past.

If by any chance Crail should get into the leaving certificate examination papers in history, or the University papers on paleography or one or other of the subjects which help to keep the Universities apart from ordinary life, one might expect questions for the testing and discomfiture of students on these lines:

Discuss the implications of the name "Carraile," under which the town was known in the ninth century.

What were the reasons that induced Margaret, the mother of Malcolm IV, to make a gift to the monks of Dryburgh of a toft of houses in the burgh of Crail?
What is a "toft of houses"?
Trace the influence of the visit of John Knox and his sermon in Crail kirk on the subsequent demolition of Popish buildings in St Andrews.
What are " Crail capons"?
By whom and in what connection were the following lines written?-

"Her wind-bleached fishers, sturdy-limbed and hale,
Her in-kneed tailors, garrulous and thin;
And some are flushed with horns of pithy ale;
And some are fierce with drams of smuggled gin,
While to augment his drouth each to his jaws
A good Crail capon holds, at which he rugs and gnaws."

Crail, by virtue of its age, has escaped town planning. There is a wide main street, with some venerable buildings. Passing downwards by some of the side streets or lanes, one discovers unexpected corner places, with engaging gable-ends, queer jumbles of buildings, reposeful nooks which have formed themselves, no one knows how. If the visitor allows himself to drift, he will eventually find himself at the harbour. The harbour also quite obviously belongs to former times. It is such a harbour as Jules Verne's little voyaging craft would like to put into.

This entire text is from *The Scotsman*, 27th August 1931.

(Opposite): Created by art students at The Waid Academy, Anstruther, in 1967, under the supervision of Principal Teacher Jimmy Selby, the magnificent mural in the school depicts the coastal villages of the East Neuk of Fife that can be seen from Kellie Law, the highest point of that portion of Fife. Each of the town murals shows the parish church steeple, the coat of arms, and aspects of the history. The Crail part of the mural shows the edible crab (partan) alongside the lobster creels. Also in the illustration are houses by the harbour and the Castle Walk.

Crail's small tidal harbour has been called the most picturesque in the East Neuk, and is fitted into the windows of thousands of digital cameras every summer.

Be in time
KY24
PETREL

(Opposite): Roger Banks surveys the North Sea from his home, Lobster Cottage, at Shoregate, overlooking Crail harbour. 'I have been terribly lucky all my life,' the Antarctic meteorologist and retired Harbourmaster of Crail says in the snug cum study of his charming home, part of which dates from the 1630s. The spacious house echoes with shades of the past. 'It was a tenement. A watchmaker's widow lived in the room we're sitting in now, and if the children were making too much noise she'd nip out of the door and whip their legs as they ran past. There were enough boys in Shoregate to form a football team.' Now many of the houses are holiday properties. The walls of Lobster Cottage are adorned with Roger's distinguished paintings of flowers and plants and, in an age of dire warnings about global warming, this wise, charming man is passionate about the preservation of the environment, and the importance of putting nutritious food into our mouths.

Crail
Harbour Gallery
and
Tearoom

Peppers

Crail Kirk dates from the second half of the 12th century, though the site is believed to have even older religious associations. After the addition of a tower to the west end, and the rebuilding of the nave, the building was dedicated to Saint Maelrubha of Applecross in Wester Ross in 1243 by David de Bernham, Bishop of St Andrews. From an early date the church belonged to the Cistercian Nunnery of St Clare in Haddington, from which it was formally disjoined in 1594. John Knox preached in Crail Kirk on his way to St Andrews in the summer of 1559 – tumultuous times in the ecclesiastical history of the nation. But this is a peaceful sanctuary, even if you only slip into a pew for a few minutes.

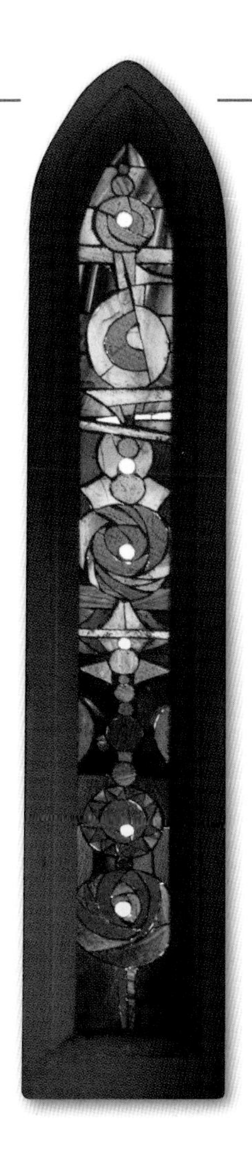

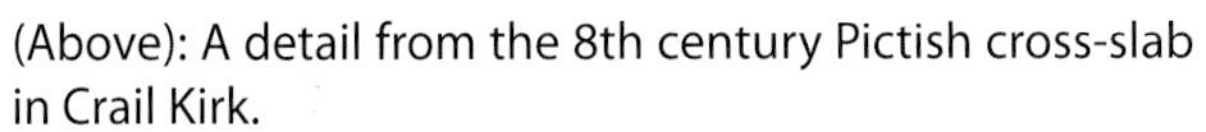

(Above): A detail from the 8th century Pictish cross-slab in Crail Kirk.

(Above right): Evocative design in the south aisle by Judith Campbell DA.

(Right): The pew frontal of principal heritor Alexander Cunningham of Barns, 1605, a splendid example of Scottish craftsmanship in oak.

(Left): Alan Gordon assists Michelle Murray (left), Ryan Petrie and Lisa Mowbray in Crail Primary School.

(Below): The chamfered square shaft of Crail's Mercat Cross dates from the early 18th century.

(Left): Who would believe that the elegant spread of St Adrians, Shoregate, Crail, was once a row of fisher folks' cottages?

The logo on the sandstone cairn erected in the Victoria Gardens Park in 2000 to mark the climax of Crail's millennium celebrations depicts the burgh's coat of arms and was executed by stonemason Alastair Aird.

In 1965 Stephen and Carol Grieve migrated from the Lake District to set up Crail Pottery, internationally appreciated for the quality of its products and their designs. Son and daughter Ben and Sarah were fired by their parents' enthusiasm and have become potters. Here Jane, Ben's wife, works on a design, a mug that could end up anywhere in the world.

(Opposite): A Raku head adorns a door at Crail Pottery. The name signifies a specialized Japanese pottery firing process which involves heating the object to a very high temperature, burning it in sawdust, then plunging it into cold water to fix the metallic glaze.

'William Beat, who wrote the old *Statistical Account* of the parish [of Kilrenny] was minister here for 37 years. His first wife - if the glowing epitaph he wrote on her marble be not overdrawn - must have been one of the chief ornaments of her sex. Probably, that was the reason why he filled her place in less than five months, and took a third wife in less than seven months after the death of the second. By a singular coincidence, George Dickson, who wrote the new *Statistical Account* of the parish, was also minister here for 37 years. The present manse was built in 1819. Conolly and Wood say that Cardinal Beaton's body was brought to Kilrenny by his cousin, and buried in the family tomb, about six yards from the east end of the church. There is better reason, however, to believe that he was buried in the Blackfriars Monastery at St Andrews. The Skeith Stone stands on a rising ground a quarter of a mile to the west of the village. On one side of this stone there is a circle about thirty inches in diameter, within which there is an eight-pointed star cross.There is no satisfactory tradition connected with this stone, and its history is quite unknown.'

David Hay Fleming, *Guide to the East Neuk of Fife*, 1886.

'"...not only few or no fish are caught, but, to the amazement of everybody, the haddocks seem to have deserted this coast; and for two years past it has become a rarity to see one." It is said that fish, even after being cooked, prefer to be swimming. Perhaps that may be one of the reasons why the 24 small brewers in Cellardyke, whom Mr Beat [author of the *Old Statistical Account*] remembered, dwindled down in his latter days "to two or three, owing to the decay of the fishery." Had he been told, in the midst of his gloomy outlook, that, in less than a century, Cellardyke was to hold a foremost place among the fishing towns of the country, that it was to have a great fleet of splendid sea-going boats, that it was to have a magnificent harbour close at hand, and that its sons would be famed for their skill and daring, the old man would have thought that it was all too good to be true...'

David Hay Fleming, *Guide to the East Neuk of Fife*, 1886.

In March 2006 a whooper swan was found floating in Cellardyke's harbour. A local resident alerted the authorities, and Britain's first case of avian influenza, caused by the H5N1 subtype, was confirmed. The world's media descended on the East Neuk port. Did the swan migrate from Iceland, Scandinavia or Northern Russia, or did it die in another country and was washed across the North Sea, to put Cellardyke on the world map for a brief notorious time?

Kilrenny and Anstruther

An old story claims that in 1616 the newly created burghs of Anstruther Wester and Anstruther Easter were ashamed to admit that they were unable to provide a butcher to make the choice cuts for a forthcoming royal visit. They could, however, have provided plenty of creels of fish, if the monarch was so disposed. Nowadays there is an adequate number of butchers in this corner of the East Neuk, and no one makes a distinction between Anstruther Wester and Easter, separated by the Dreel Burn.

If you were an Anster lad sailing into the harbour in the 16th or 17th century you would be looking out for the church spire of Anstruther Easter, and listening for the Swedish bell that was brought from Stockholm by pious merchants for whom the ring of coin was just as important as the peal from the belfry. In 1588 the Reverend James Melville was wakened rudely in his box bed to be told by a baillie: 'Ther is arryvit within our herbrie this morning a schipe full of Spainyarts, bot nocht to giff mercie bot to ask.' Next day the laird gave permission for twelve score, for the most part 'young berdless men, sillie, trauchled, and houngered' to land from the ship of the doomed Armada.

A Parochial Directory of 1862 recorded the Victorian vibrancy of Anster: 'Anstruther is one of the best fishing stations in Scotland, and fish-curing is the staple trade of the district. There are also 2 rope and sail factories, 3 oil, and 4 oilskin and fishing-gear factories, a brewery and a tannery. There is also a considerable amount of business done in the export of grain, potatoes etc. Several coasters belong to the port, and a steam-boat plies three times a week to Leith, conveying grain, fish etc., and returning with merchants' goods.'

The rope and sail factories, brewery and tannery have gone, and a steamboat no longer crosses to Leith with gentlemen in stove hats and ladies breathless in corsets. But there are still fishing vessels in the harbour at Anstruther and, in the summer, many visitors point digital cameras at the crow-stepped houses which have survived, and which now cost a king's ransom.

(Opposite): The Royal and United Burghs of Kilrenny, Anstruther Easter and Anstruther Wester are depicted in the Waid Academy mural. It includes Cellardyke, which was part of the burgh of Kilrenny, but very much a distinctive community. The mural shows the spires of the three original

The *Reaper*, a restored Fife herring drifter, the most popular design of fishing boat on the East Coast of Scotland for the greater part of the 19th and early 20th centuries, is the flagship of the Scottish Fisheries Museum, Anstruther, seen behind the stern of the boat.

Anstruther Lifeboat

The East Neuk of Fife has always had brave men willing to risk their own lives to save others at the mercy of the sea. The National Institution for the Preservation of Life was founded in 1824. Ten years later a Gold Medal was awarded to Coastguard Lieutenant Henry Randall and a Silver Medal to Coastguard Kenneth McCulloch for rescuing seven crew from the schooner *Wanderer*, wrecked at Elie in a violent storm in February 1833.

The NIPL's name was changed to the Royal National Lifeboat Institution in 1854. A station was established at Anstruther in 1865, with a boathouse built at the head of the old East Pier. The first lifeboat, *Admiral Fitzroy*, was a thirty two footer with ten oars. Six coxswains were appointed, each of them to manage the lifeboat and station for three months in turn. There were four separate crews of around a dozen men. In 1897 a hand-bell was used to summon the crew instead of a mortar or rocket signal. In 1904 a new boathouse and slipway were built. The third lifeboat on the Station was the Watson Class *James & Mary Walker*.

In 1933 the station's first motor lifeboat, the Liverpool Class *Nellie & Charles*, was delivered. In 1951 another Liverpool Class, *James & Ruby Jackson*, arrived at Anstruther. It was succeeded in 1965 by the Oakley Class *The Doctors*, then in 1991 by the Mersey Class *The Kingdom of Fife*, for which the boathouse and slipway were extended.

In 2004 a D class lifeboat was placed on service, alongside the all-weather lifeboat. The present lifeboat (seen over page on a training exercise) is a 12 Metre Mersey Class Fast Carriage Boat called *The Kingdom of Fife*.

There are over 230 lifeboat stations strategically placed around the coast of the UK, maintained through voluntary donations and the selfless dedication of unpaid crews from all walks of life. Anstruther Lifeboat is cherished by the whole community of the East Neuk. A heart-warming statistic: including all Anstruther lifeboats from 1865 to 2000, there have been over 250 lives saved.

JRC
JRC

TANG
Tang
Sula

'1655, Dec. 10, being Moneday, - all that day, for the most pairt, it did snow, bot at night ther fell extraordinar mutch snow, and all that night ther blew a great wynde, which occasioned great losse and damage to the shyre of Fyfe, both by sea and land. As for the sea, it did flow far above its [ordinar] limits and bankes... many small barkes and other vessells that perished, even laying in harbrees, as in Enster, Dysert 20, Craill 30. Also piers were doung downe in severall places, as in St Androus, Enster, Craill, Weymes, Leith; a pairt of the Salt girnell in Leven broken downe; many shipe, in severall places, overblowen by the snow and perished; some lesser houses blowen downe ; severall tries, in severall places, blowen over and broken by the violence of this storme...'

The Diary of Mr John Lamont of Newton, from the Year 1649 to the Year 1671
[*The Chronicle of Fife, Maitland Club Edition, 1830*]

Since Victorian times the lighthouse at Anstruther Harbour has been a welcome illumination for local fishermen returning from the ferocious North Sea. It was gifted by Miss Hannah Harvie of Cheltenham in 1880 in memory of Thomas Chalmers, of whom she was a devout follower. This was to mark the centenary of the great churchman's birth.

GBR

Pleasure craft have largely replaced the fishing fleet in the harbour, where Anstruther Sailing Club has access to one hundred pontoons. The Club organizes the Anstruther Muster, the largest gathering of yachts on the east coast, a weekend of fellowship and parties during which all the pontoons are in use.

One can appreciate why Anstruther waterfront is a most desirable place to live, with windows open to sea breezes.

An essential part of the history of Anstruther is contained in this atmospheric view. The white building in the foreground stands on the site of the former Dreel Castle, stronghold of the Anstruther family, on the edge of the Dreel Burn. According to tradition, Sir Philip Anstruther abandoned his castle and built a fine new mansion after King Charles II, on a visit, and having dined splendidly in Dreel Castle, remarked: 'What a fine supper I've gotten in a craw's nest!' Beyond is the steeple of the former parish church of St Adrian. George Gourlay complained bitterly in his *Anstruther or Illustrations of Scottish Burgh Life*, first published in 1888: '...the crowning deed of vandalism was in the summer of 1846, when the grand old relic was remodelled into the bare little shell you see today. The one bit of antiquity spared about the precincts is the stone coffin, in which St Adrian is said to have been buried on the Isle of May.' The church is now St Adrian's Church Hall (Hew Scott Hall) and attached to it to the left is West Anstruther Town Hall.

(Opposite): The queues outside this establishment in the evenings testify to the excellence of the product. The Smith family is a fishing dynasty. Grandfather Robert Smith OBE, fished from St Monans along with his father and brothers in the days of steam drifters, before branching out and moving to the port of Granton in Edinburgh, where he became one of the leading trawler skippers there. Robert Smith, owner of the Anstruther Fish Bar, has over a quarter of a century's experience, building up a very successful fish processing business in St Monans dealing only in fresh catches and supplying the Anstruther Fish Bar, several times winner of the coveted title of Scotland's Fish and Chip Shop of the Year.

Fish Restaurant
Awarded
of the Ye
2005
CATCH
OF THE DAY
Traditional Haddock in Batter
Local ½ Lobster
North Sea Halibut £10.10
Grilled Rainbow Trout £8.80
Icelandic Cod £8.05
Hake £6.80
NO SMOKING
WALKERS

The Scottish Fisheries Museum, Anstruther

It must be one of the biggest boathouses in the country – fishing vessels of all types and sizes, from exquisitely executed models that would fit on a mantelpiece, to a 78 foot Zulu boat. Yet from the outside it looks small, and you wonder: how have the custodians of the past managed to save so much of Scottish maritime history, when so many boats are left rotting on beaches?

The collection consists of 66,000 items, of which 74% are classified as of national, UK or international importance, and includes UK national core collection vessels. Conservation is on-going. There are so many small models of fishing vessels, accurate down to the tiniest detail, some even with a miniature crew. Some of the boats the models were made from have been sunk or broken up, so this is our only opportunity to see what they looked like three dimensionally.

The collection stretches from propulsion by oars and sail, through to the development of engines, from vessels from which a small net would have been cast by one man, to the gear used by trawlers scooping catches weighing tons from the ocean. There are the artefacts of life aboard – a brass lantern, a compass for finding home again. The whaling harpoon is a painful reminder of a method of fishing now, mercifully, in the past – almost everywhere.

The modern trawler with the pots still on the stove should perhaps have been renamed the *Marie Celeste*. The figure in the yellow oilskins in the wheelhouse is obviously anticipating a rough night, a reminder that many lives have been lost at sea. The echo-sounding equipment will track the shoal, but no technology can replace experience.

The Scottish Fisheries Museum needs at least a half day devoted to it to appreciate all its exhibits. You can even visit a typical fisherman's cottage, with a cradle in front of the cheery fire, the family awaiting the return of the father from the fishing. When you come back out into the daylight, you realise that you will never again take the fish on your plate for granted.

The window of the Memorial Room in the Scottish Fisheries Museum at Anstruther is a solemn reminder that so many failed to come home. Plaques on the wall name fishermen lost at sea since 1946, and there is a Remembrance Book in which losses before 1945 are recorded. The anchor with its connotations of a cross lying on the bottom of the ocean is a poignant symbol, composed of pieces of glass worn smooth by the action of the sea and picked up on the beaches of the East Neuk.

(Top): The *Gowanlea*, FR105, represented in this model - one of the many on display in the Scottish Fisheries Museum - was built in 1914 by Scott and Yule, Fraserburgh, for J. Strachan of Inverallochy. While operating for the Admiralty during World War I in the Adriatic, she was involved in combat with three Austrian cruisers. Skipper Joe Watt refused to surrender, so the wheelhouse was smashed, the bow damaged, the bulwarks burnt. The skipper helped to unload the dead and wounded on to another drifter and became the first fisherman to be awarded the VC. Fred Lamb, gunner of the *Gowanlea*, lost a leg but still manned the gun and was awarded the DSM. After escaping her pursuers and with the flames extinguished, the *Gowanlea* went to help other vessels in the line that were sinking. The model was made by William McDonald of Fraserburgh, grandson of Fred Lamb.

(Bottom): *Heather Bell*, BF 1206, on her first fishing trip in 1903, one of the many superb models in the Scottish Fisheries Museum. The crew is hoisting the sails and have just rigged the jib running spar, used for squaring the jib on long runs to distant fishing grounds. The model was made by Alan Whitfield, curatorial technician at the Museum, who also made the two other models of the *Heather Bell* which are on display in the Zulu Gallery. Alan does restoration/conservation work on other boat models in the collection, as well as on the full sized vessels.

The *Reaper* makes the short voyage from Anstruther to St Andrews for the 2006 St Anza Poetry Festival. The vessel was opened to the public at eight events and welcomed aboard a total of 12,235 visitors from 32 countries in addition to the United Kingdom.

(Top): An old and exhausting craft is perpetuated in the Scottish Fisheries Museum. Women came from every fishing town from Stornoway to Eyemouth to gut the massive catches of herring at Anstruther. They worked in teams of three – two gutters and a packer – at the farlan, the large wooden trough containing the herring. Strips of cloth (cloots) protected their fingers from the salt water and a slip of the razor-sharp knife. An experienced gutter could process sixty fish a minute, with £17 to £20 reckoned a good income for the backbreaking season.

The binnacle compass was a vital instrument on board steam trawlers. This one, preserved in the Scottish Fisheries Museum, was lost overboard in a gale in 1967 from the Grimsby trawler *Bombardier* off Norway. It was trawled up a year later in the same area by the *Northern Chief*.

The Waid Academy

It is appropriate that a ship putting to sea is carved on the tympanum over the main door of The Waid Academy, the largest school in the East Neuk. An Anstruther man, Lieutenant Andrew Waid (1736-1804), left his money for the founding of Waid's Orphan Naval Academy for the sons of poor mariners and fishermen. But the wishes of this generous benefactor weren't carried out, and it seems that his will was left on a shelf to gather dust, at the same time as his endowment was collecting interest. Eighty years after Waid's death, Commissioners appointed under the Educational Endowments (Scotland) Act of 1882 proposed a scheme for his money to be used for the creation of a secondary school to serve the East Neuk of Fife. In the same year their scheme was approved by the Queen in Council.

The architect David Henry produced a gabled and harled building to harmonize with local styles. On 6th September 1886 the first scholars trooped in to benefit from Lieutenant Waid's philanthropy. The first school in Scotland to be created under the 1882 Act, its constitution became a model for other schools which were created or changed as a result of the Act.

Copies of old school magazines held in The Waid Library and dating from October 1888 show a thriving school. It took until 1959 for The Waid Academy to receive a coat of arms approved by the Lord Lyon King of Arms. Appropriately, it was designed by Stewart Lees, teacher of Art at the school from 1953 to 1960. The design and motto are based on the carving in stone above the school's main door - sculpted by J. Rhind of Edinburgh. The coat of arms shows a ship passing between towers or pier heads – 'emblematical of the opening into the wide sea of life which youngsters who pass though the school may be said to be entering'. The motto is from Francis Bacon and in full it reads *Multi pertransibunt et augebitur scientia* – 'many will pass through and knowledge will be increased.' It certainly has fulfilled the pledge, judging by the number of distinguished former pupils – including Christopher Rush, the acclaimed East Neuk writer.

(Top): Generations of pupils have passed under the ship above the entrance to The Waid Academy, their passage through the school far less stormy.

(Bottom): Alex Broome and Amanda Bissett, Head Boy and Girl of The Waid Academy.

Douglas Racey, Principal Teacher of Chemistry at The Waid Academy, gets the undivided attention of his class with a spectacular combustion.

The Waid Academy pupils learning musical instruments gather for a practice with their teachers. Callum MacLeod, Principal Teacher of Music (left of picture, bearded) presides over the harmony.

Fraser Stewart and Meghan Delaney (foreground) are two cool customers in Anstruther Primary School Drama Club's production of *Guys and Dolls Jr*, the third annual show performed in 2007 by these talented children under the dedicated direction of Robert Nee.

The Guizards were formed in 1973 after a conversation was struck up between the late Derek Thirkell and the current director Sylvia Guy whilst playing a game of golf at Anstruther. The first productions were mounted in 1974, the two plays being *The Late Miss Cordell* and *The American Dream*. These were performed in Anstruther Town Hall and the group remained there for several years before moving into the Byre Theatre in St Andrews, becoming one of its top amateur groups. Sylvia Guy is the inspirational director who coaxes the cast to polished performances. The Guizards are especially keen to welcome youth into their group.

(Bottom left): The Guizards' 2007 production of *Fawlty Towers*.

Anstruther Operatic Society's 2007 production of *Anything Goes* was a resounding success. Mark you, they have had nearly 70 years of practice. The Operatic Society was founded in 1938 by Willie Blair, music master at The Waid Academy, who was inspired by the amount of talent available in Anstruther. *HMS Pinafore* was the first production, which was performed again in 1988, on the 50th anniversary of the Society. Financial arrangements for the 1938 performance were undertaken by George Doig the chemist, and Dave Jack the painter prepared the sets and scenery. There were four players in the orchestra from Anstruther, the others members from outside the town. The last night's performance was a sell-out, with 520 in the audience. The current President Elizabeth Dickson has been a member of the Operatic Society for 21 years. 'I was Hope Harcourt in this year's production of *Anything Goes*,' Elizabeth says proudly, and is looking forward to the 70th celebrations in 2008. In the photograph Elizabeth is in the third row (standing), third from the left.

(Over page): It is usually the exterior of Buckie House, Anstruther, that pedestrians – and drivers – admire as they come along High Street. The east gable of the house, built in 1692, is decorated with rows of scallop shells and buckies (whelks) stuck on by the eccentric slater and joiner Alexander Batchelor in the mid 19th century. But the interior, and particularly the Grotto Room, is equally appealing. Its ceiling and window embrasures are adorned with cream and brown shells from the East Neuk. Batchelor hung out a notice for visitors: 'Here is the famous Grotto Room/ The like's not seen in any toun:/Those who do it wish to see, /It's only threepence asked as fee.' For an extra penny you could see Batchelor in his own shell-covered coffin. It is not known if he was buried in it when he died in 1866. Anne Morris is the careful custodian of this unique example of East Neuk artistry by a man who went down on his knees on a twenty mile stretch of coastline to search for suitable shells.

The Esplanade, leading to the shore at Anstruther, is a shady walk of historic houses. The crow-stepped building on the right is a former inn, with a wheatsheaf panel inset in the wall. On the left hand side, there is the old manse of 1703, and further up, The Shipmaster's House.

Witchcraft

Witches were credited with the power of raising storms and threatening boats, which is perhaps why they were particularly feared in the East Neuk of Fife. But was this a good reason for the barbaric way in which Janet Cornfoot was treated by a Pittenweem mob in January 1705? 'They fell upon the poor creature and beat her unmercifully,' a chronicler recorded, 'tying her so hard with a rope that she was almost strangled. They dragged her through the streets and along the shore by her heels, stretched a rope between a ship and the shore to a great height, to which they tied her fast, after which they swung her to and fro from one side to another, in the meantime throwing stones at her until they were weary. Then they loosened her, and with a mighty swing threw her upon the hard sands, all about being ready in the meantime to receive her with stones and staves, with which they beat her most cruelly. They laid a heavy door upon her, with which they pressed her so sore that she cried out to let her up for Christ's sake and she would tell the truth. But when they did let her up what she said could not satisfy them, and therefore they again laid on her the door, and with a heavy weight of stones on it pressed her to death; and to be sure that it was so they called a man with a horse and sledge and made him drive over her corpse backwards and forwards several times.'

But as St Andrews University lecturer Dr Peter Maxwell-Stuart, a leading authority on witchcraft in Scotland, author of *An Abundance of Witches: The Great Scottish Witch-Hunt*, and *Satan's Conspiracy: Magic and Witchcraft in Sixteenth Century Scotland*, cautions, the Pittenweem incident was extremely unusual, and very few witches were subject to the summary 'justice' of the mob. In fact, as he points out: '... when witches came to trial, their assizes seem to have done their best to listen to the evidence presented, and to pass their verdict in accordance with that evidence, so that perhaps (although I expect not without controversy) we may say of some of them at least what Increase Mather said of the judges and jurors at Salem, that "they are good and wise men, and have acted with all fidelity according to their light."'

Andrew Sherriff is well protected against unwelcome visitors from the past as he sits in the ingle neuk of his house at Shore Street, Anstruther, which he purchased in 1983. During the property's renovation the fireplace above, hidden since the late 18th century, was uncovered. The wooden beam forming the lintel had unusual markings on it (see photograph opposite). Andrew's researches have led him to conclude that these are apotropaic markings, supposedly having the power to avert evil or bad luck in a property. Were they made on the lintel to protect the inhabitants against the witches of Anstruther? Andrew says: 'The markings in my house are the most significant so far found in Scotland. I have located markings in other buildings, namely the Palace at Culross, Craigievar Castle and Provost Skene's House in Aberdeen. In all cases I informed the guardians of these properties that they had something that should be preserved.' Andrew's interest in the subject was inspired by the researches of Timothy Easton into ritual or apotropaic marks found on timbers and used to evoke Christ or Mary to protect the building's occupants from witchcraft and evil.

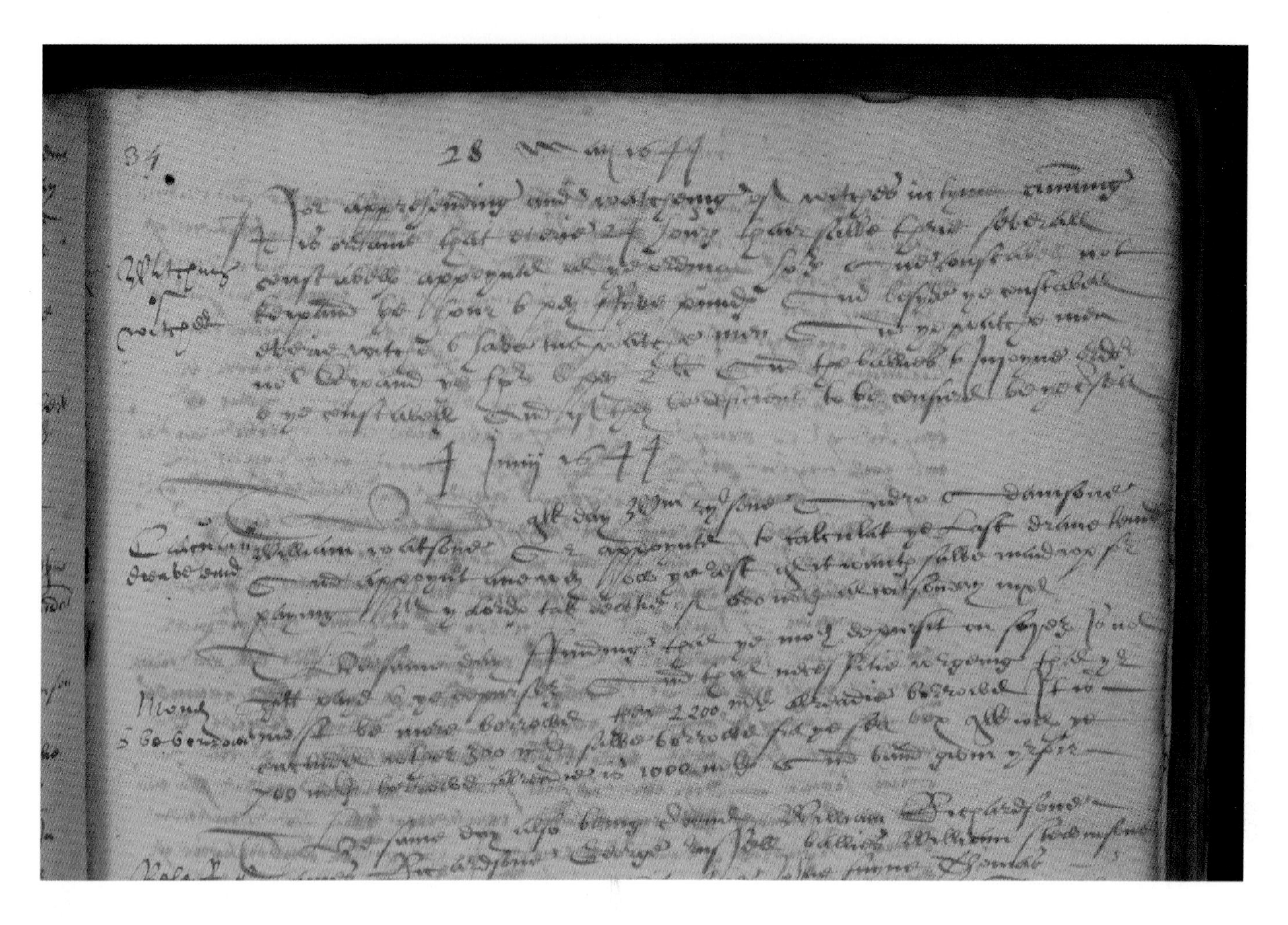

(Top): 28 Mai 1644: 'For apprehending and watcheing of witches in tyme cum[m]ing It is ordanit that everyie 24 hours thaer salbe thrie severall constabells appoyntit at ye ordinar ho[u]rs and constabels not keipand the hour to pey ffyve punds And besyde ye constabell everie witche to have tuo watche men And ye watche men no[ch]t keipand ye ho[u]r to pey 2 Lib And the ballies to Injoyne ordo[u]r to ye constabell And if they be deficient to be censured be the c[on]sell.'

From the *Minute book of Burgh of Pittenweem*, 1629-1727, in the Library of the University of St Andrews.

This small primitive doll with pages from the Bible was discovered by Andrew Sherriff in his Anstruther house. It had been hidden along with ears of corn, dried peas, wine corks and a small glass bottle with a broken neck. It is suspected that the doll might not have been purely defensive against the evil allegedly perpetrated by witches, but might have had a role in the placing of curses.

Christine Crow stands next to her ironic self-portrait in which she is holding a miniature Bass Rock – one of her adopted painterly emblems - in the company of her 'Crow' familiar, a creature made of writerly quills. A former lecturer in French Literature at the University of St Andrews, Christine is the author of several books on the poetry and thought of the French writer Paul Valéry. Moving to Anstruther in 1994 in order to write poetry and fiction, she found herself turning into a painter as well. Although her paintings have been exhibited to critical approval, Christine prefers to see herself as a creative hermit in her 'Sitooterie' studio on the edge of the North Sea. Christine's husband, Liverpool-born John Amson, retired mathematics lecturer at the University of St Andrews and authority on navigation, set up a small business pioneering personal computer software for navigation. His Tide Prediction programs were the first ever to be made commercially available in Europe and have been widely used by merchant and national navies and coastal engineering companies. John has now turned to devising ingenious ways of improving the predictive accuracy of mechanical Tide Clocks of the kind that were often made to order by the Anstruther and Pittenweem clockmakers for successful East Neuk fishing families in the 19th century.

Bill Flett is one of the best well-kent characters in the East Neuk. This self-effacing son of Anstruther has been taking photographs for the *Courier* newspaper for more years than he cares to calculate. It is appropriate that he is pictured beside a bus, as this is his sole means of conveyance, yet he has never missed a photo shoot. Below is one of his classic photographs - boys making a splash in Anstruther harbour.

(Opposite): Why are these trees on the road out of Anstruther to St Andrews known locally as the African trees?

Pittenweem

Pittenweem has existed ever since man began to fish the Fife coast with the most rudimentary gear. A possible derivation of its name (*pit*, farm, and *uamh*, cave, probably after St Fillan's Cave) suggests its agricultural background. But it was also a place where the soul as well as the soil was tended. A Benedictine Priory was transferred to Pittenweem from the Isle of May in 1318.

Around the time that the town became a Royal Burgh in 1541, the outer pier was constructed. In 1771 Sir John Anstruther had the substantial inner pier built. The west pier was added in the 19th century to complete the safe harbour we see today. Round it shipbuilders, fishermen and brewers with faith in the place built houses which are still occupied, though, instead of a telescope on a window sill to watch for a returning schooner, there is likely to be a satellite box. Gyles House, on the edge of the harbour, is the former home of the 'other' Captain Cook, who assisted in the flight of Charles II to France in 1651.

An unwelcome visitor to Pittenweem in 1779 was the privateer John Paul Jones. The Scottish born so-called 'Father of the American Navy' anchored half a mile off Pittenweem in the USS *Bonhomme Richard*. Despite bombarding Anstruther, Jones did not attack Pittenweem, but did make off with the town's pilot who had sailed out to meet the invader.

Pittenweem's narrow ways through which the wind from the North Sea funnels echo with the rumble of smugglers' barrels, the screams of burning witches. Cove Wynd; Water Wynd; Calman's Wynd – names that resonate with history, with the sound of returning sea boots, exotic toys in the bag for excited children, the scuffle of slippers as a servant girl grants a kiss before going indoors to prepare a supper of produce from the sea. But through these wynds to the cemetery were carried the corpses of the drowned, because this is a dangerous as well as a beautiful stretch of coast.

Let us hope that the name of the inner boat tied up at Pittenweem harbour is fulfilled at the fishing grounds.

UO - VARDIS
JUST REWARD

'As the harbour is mentioned in the days of William the Lion, it may therefore be inferred that the town [Pittenweem] was of some note seven centuries ago, both as a trading seaport and a place of fishing. At the end of July 1559, John Knox and Robert Hamilton sailed from this port to Holy Island, to meet Sir Harry Percy. Before 1639, there belonged to the town at least "13 sail of large vessels; all of which were either taken by the enemy, wrecked, or sold in consequence of the death of the commanders and mariners at the battle of Kilsyth." Nor did the harbour escape the violence of the terrible storm of the 10th December 1655; for it is mentioned in the Minutes of the Synod of Fife that when the Provincial Assembly met at St Andrews, on the 7th of April 1657, a petition was presented from the town of Pittenweem, desiring a recommendation for charitable assistance from the kirks of the province, towards the repairing of their harbour, which was ruined by that storm.'

David Hay Fleming, *Guide to the East Neuk of Fife*, 1886.

RESIDENTS ONLY
RESIDENTS ONLY

If I change with all the winds that blow,
It is only because they made me so,
And people would think it wondrous strange,
If I, a Weathercock, should not change.

Henry Wadsworth Longfellow (1807-1882)

Pittenweem Primary School pupils with their dedicated teachers and support staff.

James More Horsburgh was born in Hartlepool, where his father found work in the herring industry, but they returned to Pittenweem. At The Waid Academy nobody seems to have noticed the boy's remarkable gift for painting. Art School was a luxury beyond his dreams, and he spent most of his life fishing out of Pittenweem in yawls, where sleeping below deck was a brief cramped experience miles out in the rolling North Sea. Part of the summer was spent fishing out of the Isle of Man. 'Painting was always a hobby for me,' More recalls. Weekends on shore were for catching up with family news. When there was time and money for his hobby, it never occurred to him to try to sell his paintings. The meticulous brushwork of reconstructing from memory the fishing yawls was sufficient reward, especially when this chronicler of the Pittenweem fishing fleet points out that all of the figures in the boats are actual people he fished beside.More's paintings first came to the attention of the public in a show at the harbour organised by the Pittenweem Arts Festival, and became so prized that one year people were sitting on the steps of the venue, waiting for the show to open. Now you can buy prints of these exquisite records of fishing. (As this book was being prepared for the press James More Horsburgh died, mourned by family, friends, and many admirers of his art).

J M HORSBURGH.

In Pittenweem time means nothing to a terrier.

Now several metres above sea level, St Fillans Cave at Cove Wynd, Pittenweem, would have been at sea level millennia ago and was probably carved out by the action of the ocean. The cave has traditionally been associated with St Fillan, although there are stories of several saints with that name from the area. Ages after the saint's passing the cave was probably used by local fishermen to store their gear, or even to shelter from storms. The cave, which is owned by the Bishop Low Trust, and entrusted to St John's Scottish Episcopal Church in Pittenweem, was refurbished and opened to visitors in 2000. Please respect the silence and spiritual aura of the cave which is still a place of pilgrimage.

Torches light the way in procession at Pittenweem Arts Festival, which had its origins in 1981, when an exhibition of old photographs of the town was presented in aid of Lifeboat funds at Kellie Lodgings, one of Pittenweem's oldest houses. The response inspired three artists then living in Pittenweem to establish a Pittenweem Arts Festival the following year. It aimed to show high-quality exhibitions of visual arts and to include evening performances of drama, music and poetry. The first invited artist was Ian Hamilton Finlay, with his exhibition *Diamond Studded Fishnets* based on fishing boats and boat names. The first Festival was entitled A Pittenweem Fancy, using the old term 'fancy,' meaning a celebration. Since then Pittenweem Arts Festival has become an essential annual visit for those interested in the arts, and distinguished names are proud to exhibit and perform in the East Neuk town.

Having graduated from Edinburgh University in 1989, Kenny Anderson (on the right: (aka King Creosote) and son of Fife accordion virtuoso Billy Anderson), spent two years busking with an accordion around Europe before bringing his band Skuobhie Dubh Orchestra to Scotland. When the SDO disbanded in 1996, Kenny started a solo project - King Creosote - on his own Fence Records label, based in Fife, and over the next ten years built up the Fence Collective by running regular music nights in his home town of St. Andrews. In 1995 King Creosote signed up with 679 Recordings, releasing the acclaimed *KC Rules OK*, followed by *Bombshell*. Johnny Lynch (aka the Pictish Trail) joined the Fence Collective in 2003, having graduated from St. Andrews University, and is now label manager of Fence Records. He also runs his own music promotions and distribution company Trailerpark. He plays electric guitar and sings with the King Creosote live band, and somehow finds time to organize his own band shows between KC tours. These two formidably talented musicians, who are tipped for the big time, organize the Homegame Festival, already in its sixth year, which brings bands and music fans from all over Britain to Anstruther.

Adrienne McStay brought her golden apples to Pittenweem Arts Festival. Dublin born, a student at the Pilchuck Glass School, Washington, Adrienne has worked in glass studios in Copenhagen, Seattle, Washington and Edinburgh. In 1993 she established A. McStay Glass Blowing Studio at Newport-on-Tay in Fife. She has exhibited throughout the UK and the USA. Adrienne points out that glass-making in Scotland has a long and distinguished history, beginning in Fife during the early years of the 17th century. Unlike mass-producing glass factories, Adrienne's studio creates unique glass pieces to innovative designs, work inspired by the colours of nature and the nature of hot flowing glass. Her artistic manifesto is clear: 'My eyes see nature all around. They see beauty in the smallest detail - a fallen leaf or on a larger scale, the quality of light passing through a landscape. It is the essence of nature that I try to capture in my work.'

(Opposite): Fife artist Marie Louise Wrightson, who exhibited her work at the Pittenweem Arts Festival, explains the symbolism of the swan and the stand of cakes: 'One of my own strong beliefs is the commitment to wildlife conservation. So, in my work the saint is represented by a bird. For example St Elizabeth is the patron saint of bakers, because she fed the poor with bread. Each bird has a story to tell and by looking through the painting a message is there for personal interpretation. Some of the objects that I have used have been chosen for their kitsch feel, the Christmas cracker toys, the 1960s glass and the traditional tin of biscuits. I have brought these three elements together, the saints, conservation through birds and modern kitsch objects. I hope to awaken the viewer to conservation through vivid colour, highly detailed imagery and an opportunity to let the imagination wander from an observational stance.'

St Monans

Edinburgh, March 16, 1893.

SIR,- In "The East Neuk of Fife: Its History and Antiquities," second edition, p.232, Mr Wood speaks of "the Culdee preacher, Monan... who was murdered by the Danes in 874." At p.7 of the same work, the following quotation from "Wynton's Chronicle" is given:-

"At Invereye St Monance.
That of the company was ane,
Chusit him so near the sea
To lead his life: thair endit he."

The origin and meaning of the name are thus seen. And it is evident that the correct spelling is that which contains the suggestion of history, not that which is merely sufficient to indicate the sound of the word. It is St Monan's [town]. Would any one ever think of writing "St Andrewce" or "St Johnce"?

The tendency to revert to the correct form is becoming noticeable, and surely it would be easy to establish it once for all, as was done some years ago in the case of Duns, formerly Dunse. – I am, &c,

John Turnbull.

P.S.-It so happens that I bear the name of the parish minister of St Monans. I do not wish to make him responsible for this letter.

SIR, - I hope you will persevere in spelling St Monans properly, till you have educated Fife folk out of the illiterate and vulgar blunder of writing St Monance.

St Monan of Scotland, martyr, died 874. Of course the place called after him is St Monans. If you write St Monance, you ought, of course, to write, St Andrewce, St Albance, St Davidce, St Valentince, St Swithince, St Stephence, St Kentigernece. – I am,

K.

The Scotsman, 17th March, 1893.

(Opposite): The Waid Academy mural depicts the two main industries of St Monans – boatbuilding and fishing, with the oilskinned duo hauling in the net. The parish church by the sea is in the background.

MARE VIVIMUS
KY.

'In the Annual Report of the Fishery Board for Scotland, for 1883, it is stated that:- "The fishermen of St Monance, to their great credit, unaided by any public grant, erected a good harbour there, at a cost of about £15,000. The increased size of the boats now engaged in the fisheries rendered it absolutely necessary that some rock should be excavated, and the outer entrance channel to the harbour widened, but the fishermen were quite unable to raise the amount required for these additional works. After having made full enquiry into the whole circumstances of the case, we resolved that, in the event of the fishermen paying us £500, we would expend an amount not exceeding £2000 in all towards carrying out what was required. This £500 was sent to us, and we had the gratification of ordering the works to be proceeded with." A year earlier the Board reported that on the whole east coast of Scotland there were only four really good harbours for fishing boats, namely, those at Aberdeen, Peterhead, Fraserburgh, and Cluny harbour at Buckie.'

David Hay Fleming, *Guide to the East Neuk of Fife*, 1886.

KY 450

KY 450

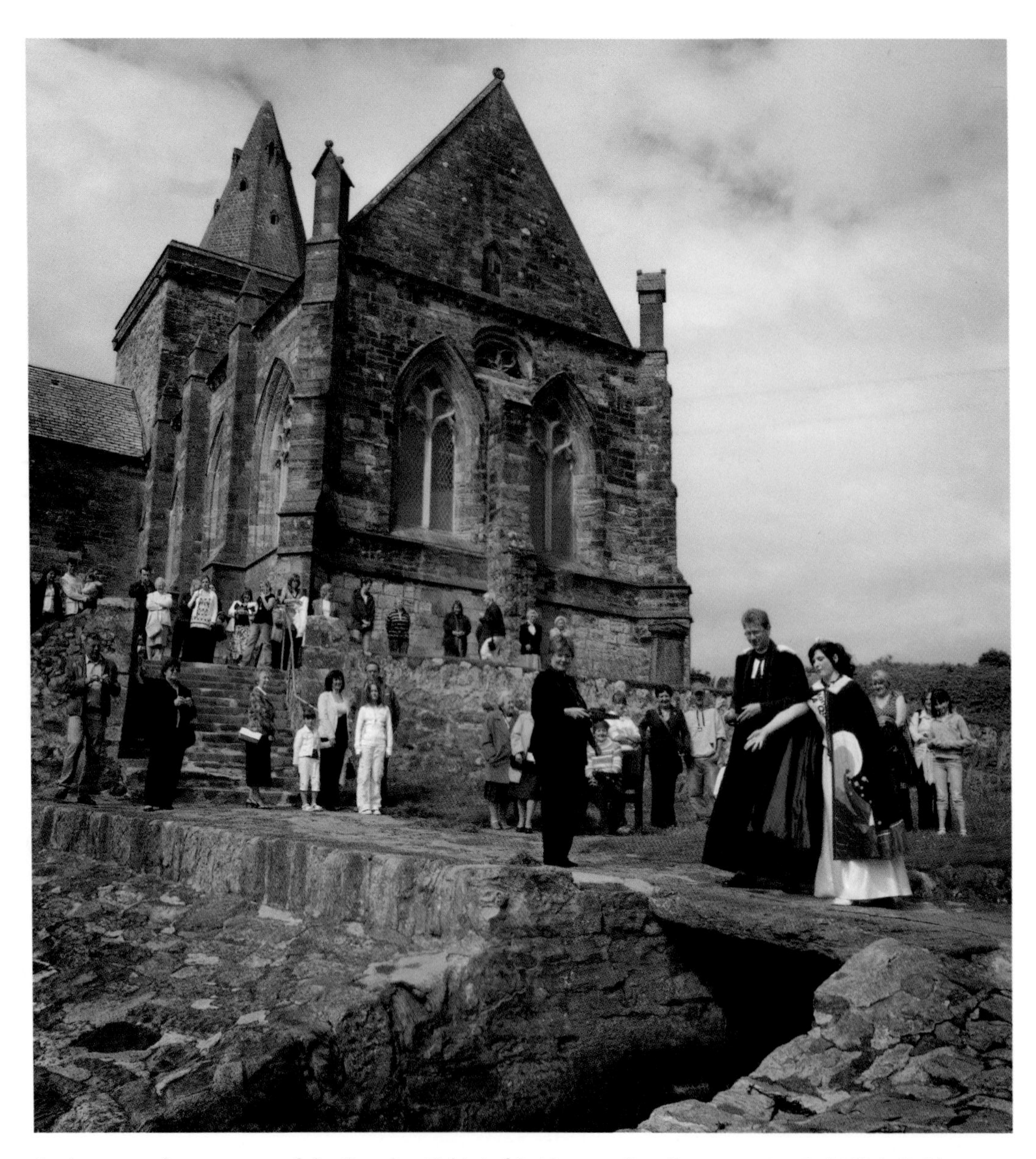

At the annual ceremony of the Sunday Kirkin' of St Monans Sea Queen at the Auld Kirk, St Monans, the Reverend Dr Donald MacEwan and Jena Morris stand on the Inverie burn brig. In former years the Sea Queen had a family connection with the sea - father, grandfather, or brother, a fisherman, or other maritime activity. The Sea Queen's family had to arrange a fishing boat for the 'royal' party to travel in. Nowadays the Sea Queen and her entourage sail from Anstruther on the Scottish Fisheries Museum's *Reaper*.

(Opposite): The construction of the Auld Kirk, St Monans, was paid for in 1362-70 by David II, who endowed it as a chapel. In 1471 James III transferred the chapel and endowments to the Dominicans. In 1647 the choir was blocked off for public worship, and became a parish church in 1649. Roofless towards the end of the 18th century, the abandoned transepts were restored by William Burn in 1826-28, when the entire building was brought back into public use. The two model boats hung in the north and south crossing arches show how the congregation relied for a living from the sea, and at the same time sought protection from it through prayer. The south crossing model boat was donated in 1805 by a local mariner, Captain Marr, and paid for by the prize money he had received while commanding a ship of the line under Nelson in the Napoleonic campaign. The north crossing model, donated in the 19th century, is of a steam drifter, *Pursuit*.

Tim Hacking and Bonnie McKenzie chose St Monans Auld Kirk for their wedding on 28th July 2007.

Katie O'Donnell and Steven Handley are happy to exchange their classroom in St Monans Primary School for the kitchen of the Seafood Restaurant in the same town. Pupils are invited to the restaurant each year as part of the school's Enterprise Programme so that they can get some experience of the world of work, at the same time picking up tips about healthy eating. The chef demonstrating the skills of his profession is Andy Simpson.

(Over page): These former fishermen's houses at West Shore, St Monans, were in a ruinous condition after World War II, but were acquired by the National Trust for Scotland, renovated and sold to individuals. The door on the left will lead you back in time, courtesy of the St Monans Heritage Collection. You can view a selection of the thousands of photographs taken by local shopkeeper William Easton in the early 1900s when St Monans was thriving through herring fishing. You can also see the clothes these hardy men wore, and the nets they cast in freezing seas.

ST. MONANS HERITAGE
COLLECTION
5

Half a mile west of St Monans, the ruins of Newark Castle are vulnerable to the storms that can sweep up the Forth. Like some other Scottish castles, dating its construction is difficult, but the 15th century seems likely for the earliest part. The house was extended in the late 16th century, including the addition of gunloops. In 1649 the castle was bought by Sir David Leslie, who was made Lord Newark in 1661. The remains include vaulted cellars, part of a tower block, a partially collapsed round tower, and fragments of the outer walls on the coast. In his indispensable illustrated architectural guide, *The Kingdom of Fife* Glen L. Pride records that Newark's ruins were 'once subject of abortive restoration schemes by Sir Robert Lorimer, for Sir William Burrell in 1898-9.' Had these schemes been carried out, the East Neuk might have shared the Burrell spoils with Glasgow.

(Over page): On the outskirts of St Monans this recently restored windmill, dating from around 1780, was used in the extraction of sea salt from salt pans.

lie and Earlsferry

'Two burghs joining hands round a natural harbour': that is how the eloquent and informed architectural historian John Gifford describes Elie and Earlsferry in his seminal study of Fife in the Buildings of Scotland series. It is claimed that MacDuff, Earl of Fife, crossed the Forth there in 1054 while fleeing from King Macbeth, and that Earlsferry received its name because in the 12th century the Earls of Fife instituted a ferry across the Firth of Forth to North Berwick for the benefit of pilgrims en route to the shrine of Saint Andrew the Apostle at St Andrews.

Earlsferry was elevated to a royal burgh in 1541, and in 1589 Elie became a burgh of barony under the control of the lairds of Ardross. Elie's single pier was rebuilt and lengthened around 1855. The nearby railway, built in 1857, was extended through Elie to Anstruther in 1863 and brought Victorian tourists from the congested unhealthy cities, for a break of bracing air and restorative views.

Visitors began to look for holiday homes in Elie, leading to a building boom. Club makers in the burgh supplied the craze for golf. Elie and Earlsferry were formally merged in 1930, but though they share shops and other amenities, have retained their identities, a strong sense of individual history. The railway line was broken up under the Beeching axe in the 1960s, but the era of the family car had arrived.

Elie brides now travel by chauffeur-driven limousine and are not carried along in a barrel, as happened to the maiden who underwent a secret marriage to the coxswain of the Duke of York's barge when that nobleman visited Elie in his capacity as Governor of Scotland. It was the minister at Kilconquhar who arranged the marriage, following which the bride was smuggled aboard the Duke's barge in a barrel. The inquisitive who enquired about the contents of the barrel (perhaps hoping for a free libation) were informed: 'It's but a swan from Kilconquhar Loch, to be taken to Holyrood.' The episode inspired a ballad, with a muffled voice emerging from the barrel: 'And it's fare-ye-weel my father's house/And Elie evermore.'

(Opposite): The Waid Academy mural shows the scene at Elie and Earlsferry with two sailing dinghies. The facilities now include windsurfing, kayaking and water skiers being towed behind speedboats alongside the dinghy sailors.

131
98
W

'[Elie] is described, in Chambers' *Gazetteer of Scotland*, as "an ancient little town of no trade," and as "excessively dull." But though it is nine and thirty years more ancient now, it is certainly not excessively dull. It is a delightfully quiet retreat, for those who wish to escape from the din and bustle of the city, to rusticate where they can enjoy the combined advantages of a sea-side resort and country town. The streets are wide and clean, the air is clear and bracing, the beach is splendid for bathing, the rocks are wild and rugged, the water supply is abundant and excellent, there are many beautiful walks and drives in the neighbourhood, and the golfing links of Earlsferry are close at hand. There is an "Elie Golf-House Club," an "Earlsferry and Elie Golf Club," and also a Cricket Club, a Lawn-Tennis Club, and a Curling Club. As Elie is likewise easy of access by rail, road, and sea, it is sure to rise much higher in popular esteem.'

David Hay Fleming, *Guide to the East Neuk of Fife*, 1886.

Graham Pollock and daughter Lois on a memorable day at Elie Church on 12th August 2006.

'How's that?' Elie Cricket Club's fixtures depend, not on rain but on tide. Their pitch is the beach by the harbour, with matches lasting for sixty overs. Each player other than the two wicket keepers must bowl three overs with a windball, an indoor cricket ball made of rubber with a rubber seam. Once the stumps are drawn they repair to their pavilion, the Ship Inn Pub.

The children of Elie Primary School get a lesson in aerobics. Or are they cheering because they have been granted an extra holiday?

The wave-cut platform of Kincraig Point was formed from volcanic ash. Once the land had stabilized, the sea began to erode it to its present dramatic shape, creation's giant footprint in the Firth of Forth.

(Opposite): In 1929 a group of Elie and Earslferry residents, who wished to make the shoreline around Kincraig Point more accessible to the public, raised one hundred pounds by public subscription and commissioned a local blacksmith to install posts and chains, and to carve footholds in the volcanic rock. The Chain Walk has been called more of a scramble than a walk, but is a safe and interesting way to view the coastline for the fit.

On 10th June 1940, the day that Mussolini declared war on France and Britain, an Italian ship about to leave Methil Docks decided to make a run for it. But the Captain didn't know about the naval guns installed in concrete emplacements on top of the 200 foot high Kincraig Cliffs. During target practice the windows of the houses in Elie and Earlsferry were threatened by the concussion of the naval guns, the shells so large that the naked eye could track them in flight. When the Italian ship was right abeam of Earlsferry, the big guns opened fire. The first shell landed half a mile in front of the ship's bow, the second a quarter of a mile in front. The ship didn't slow. But when the third shell landed a few feet in front of its bow the ship shuddered to a halt and surrendered. The first – and last – engagement of the Kincraig naval guns had ended in victory.

(Opposite): Berwick Law across the Firth of Forth rears through spume breaking on Elie shore. The Law is composed of igneous rock formed during the early carboniferous era, in an area which was the site of many volcanic eruptions. The Law is the result of the mouth of the volcano being choked with its own molten lava, forming a plug when extinct.

On the east side of Elie Ness, at Ruby Bay, are the remains of the Lady's Tower, built in the 1770s as a changing room for the use of Lady Jane Anstruther. When she wanted a dip the modest Jane first sent a bell ringer around Elie to let the residents know they should keep away from Ruby Bay. This was the same lady who is reputed to have had a whole settlement moved to improve the view from her house, leading to a curse being placed on the family. But where was this settlement, and did the curse work? Ruby Bay is named after Elie rubies, actually a type of garnet, which are sometimes found here.

Elie Lighthouse, beacon for homeward-bound East Neuk mariners.

Built by the last of the Stevenson lighthouse builders, David and Charles Stevenson, in 1908, the 36 foot high Elie Lighthouse is still in use guiding shipping in the outer parts of the Forth. However, the purists complain that it has lost its distinctive glass lantern house and sloping copper roof and weather vane. There is a local legend of a lady artist who used to carry her easel out to the lighthouse every summer to paint the structure as it was, before the acetylene flame that generated the light beam was replaced by an electric bulb strobe light.

Erected in 1819-21, Kilconquhar Parish Church was based on Richard Crichton's design of 1818 for Cockpen Church, Lothian. This does not detract from its peaceful charm in one of the most alluring and stylish villages in the East Neuk, its castle, a late 16th century tower augmented by Victorian additions by William Burn and David Bryce, fashionable architects of castles and mansions. Kilconquhar Castle is now a popular timeshare and leisure resort.

(Over page): The Bass Rock looms from the site of Largo House, 'desolate shell of a grand classical mansion,' as Glen L. Pride notes sadly in *The Kingdom of Fife*.

St Adrian, who had his habitation on the Isle of May in the Firth of Forth in the 7th century, must have had his prayers interrupted many times by the clamour of seabirds. In 1934 Scotland's first bird observatory was established on the island, and is now under the protective care of Scottish Natural Heritage. The main lighthouse was designed in 1816 by the engineer Robert Stevenson (of Robert Louis's family) and operated until 1989, when the last keepers left the island. You can travel out to the island on *May Princess* (below) – weather permitting, of course.

As it waddles past its burrow on the Isle of May, the puffin, with its large red feet and multi-coloured bill, looks likes a brightly painted mechanical toy. At the last five yearly count in 2003 there were 68,000 puffins on the island, but the colony may be vulnerable in future to scarcity of sand eels and the effects of climate change.

Herring gulls and seals inhabit the rocks and coves of the Isle of May.

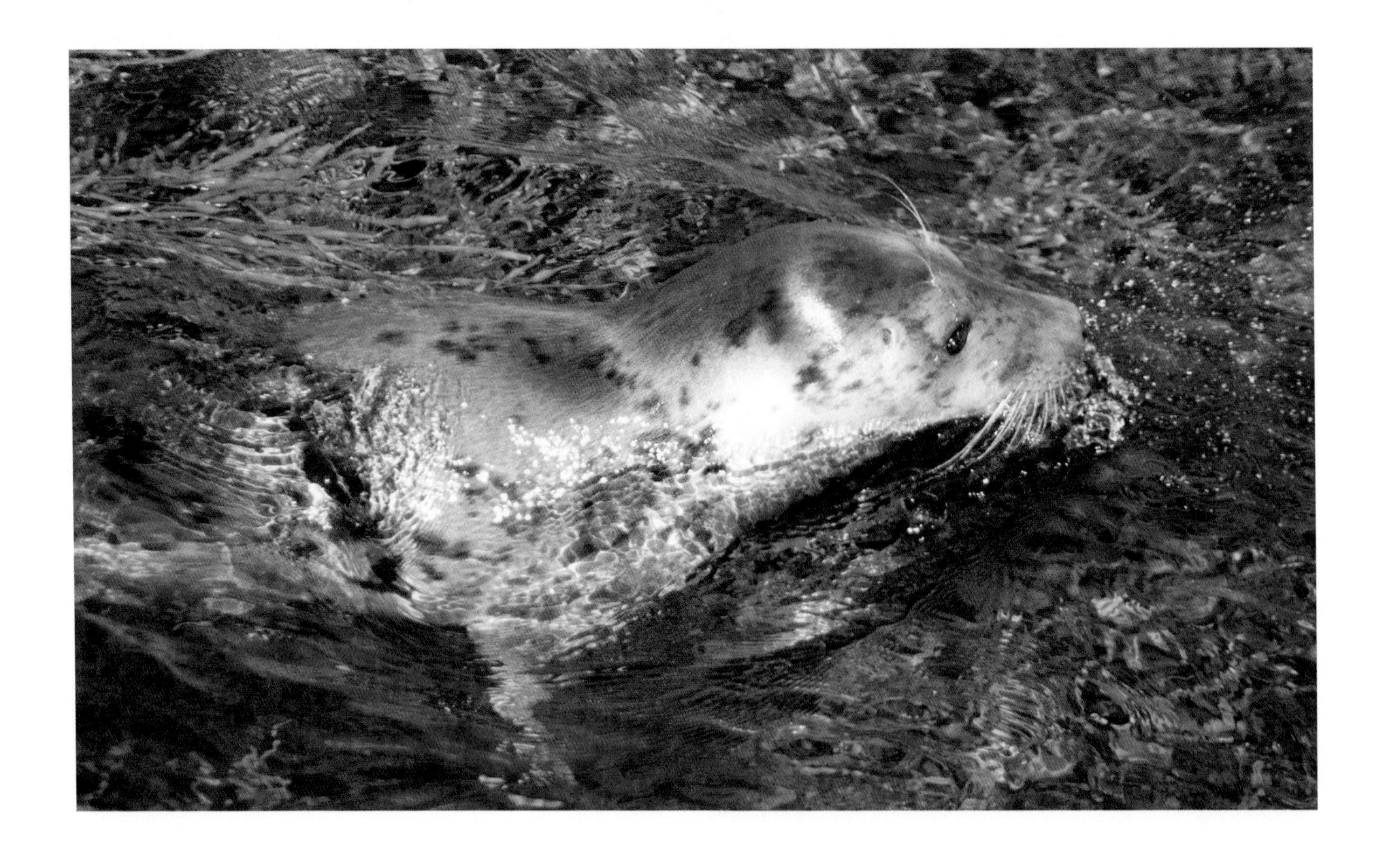

Ann Cairns from Boarhills has brought the exotic to the East Neuk of Fife in the elegant form of her Portuguese horse Chiquela as they dance across the paddock at Ovenstone Equine just outside Pittenweem. 'I've been interested in dressage ever since I started riding at age 12, but only since I retired have I really had the time and opportunity to find out more and work hard at acquiring the skills,' Ann says, explaining that the word dressage is derived from the French and 'just means training the horse.' Up until the 18th century the horse was trained in the methods still used by the Spanish Riding School. In those unruly times it was regarded as a weapon in war, able to undertake long marches, but still fit enough for the rider to show off his skills to the ladies. This training survives in Spain and Portugal. 'The clothes I'm wearing and the saddle and bridle I have is the typical formal or parade dress of Portuguese riders,' Ann explains. 'Women riders wear either a wide full-length skirt or culottes, as I do. The lady's hat differs from the man's in having two black silk pom-poms on the brim at the left.The jacket is tailored and quite stiff but very comfortable to wear. The saddle is very like the one used in the American West which was developed from the Spanish and Portuguese saddles of the early settlers.' In the photograph Ann is performing a movement called *piaffe*, best described as a very energetic, highly rhythmical trot virtually on the spot. There must be a definite moment of suspension when the horse is in the air between each stride.

Scotland's Secret Bunker

In the late 1950s the farmhand walking his plough horses to a show wouldn't have given the traditional East Neuk farmhouse a second glance, but underneath the building was a command centre capable of directing the governance of Scotland in the event of a nuclear attack, the phobia of the post-war world following Hiroshima and Nagasaki. The civil engineering project to construct the bunker was awesome. A 40-metre deep cavity with a shock-absorbing foundation of gravel had to be excavated. The outer shell of the building was constructed with three metres of solid concrete reinforced with thick tungsten rods. The guardhouse was built to resemble a traditional Scottish farmhouse but secretly reinforced with concrete and steel girders. This building concealed the access to the bunker and provided accommodation for the security guards who would have watched our ploughman passing to his show.

But who was to occupy this underground construction? Senior ministers would be evacuated here from Edinburgh, along with their key civil servants. The offices of the emergency services, scientific advisors, the Met Office and computer staff would surround the main command floor. On the main floor senior staff from the major ministries would keep in touch with the outside world and up-to-the-minute status information would be shown on the giant map displays and wall charts. The final three minute warning would be received on the telephones in the Operations Room.

Suppose the siren has gone, and the Soviet missile is on its way: how is contaminated air to be kept out of the command bunker? The Plant Room was capable of moving 1500 cubic metres of air every minute, in effect changing the entire air content of the bunker every fifteen minutes. In the event of a power failure the bunker had its own emergency generator that could produce 750kva for up to three months - enough to supply the coastal villages in Fife. The switchboards were staffed by ten operators twenty four hours a day.

But why give away any more secrets? Go and see for yourself this absorbing subterranean relic of the Cold War, and be thankful that it was never utilized.

Lifelike models in Scotland's Secret Bunker plot a course for survival.

Kellie Castle

That 'glorious first of September in 1878' when he carried a candle upstairs to his bed in Kellie Castle, fourteen year old Robert Lorimer wouldn't have questioned his father's sanity (as did some of the neighbours) for taking a thirty eight year lease on the castle as a summer holiday home. The teenager would have regarded it as a great adventure to be living in a building locals regarded as a ruin, with its broken windows, leaking roofs, fireplaces choked with the fallen nests of long-dead jackdaws and rooks. The condition of Kellie, and the possibility of restoring it must have fired the creative imagination of the teenager who would become one of Scotland's finest architects.

Was the young Robert's sleep ever disturbed by the restless footsteps of a Siward, a relation of the Earl of Northumberland who had led an invasion of Scotland in 1054 during the reign of Macbeth? The Oliphants came next. In 1573 a new tower was built by the 4th Lord Oliphant to the east of the original tower. In 1613 Kellie Castle became the property of Sir Thomas Erskine, Earl of Mar, who had saved the life of King James VI during the Gowrie Conspiracy. The king stayed at Kellie in 1617 during his only visit to Scotland after the Union of the Crowns, and rewarded his host with the title of Earl of Kellie. The Earldom of Kellie became extinct in 1829, and thereafter jackdaws and rooks were the only tenants until Professor James Lorimer signed the long lease in 1878.

From his restoration work on Kellie the Professor's son Robert developed a passion for the Scottish Baronial style which he was to reproduce, in adapted form, in other buildings. Kellie Castle's interior and some of its furnishings bear the stamp of his genius, and his son Hew inherited his father's fascination for stone, working as an internationally respected sculptor at Kellie until he sold the castle and gardens to the National Trust for Scotland in 1970.

The Trust has been Kellie Castle's careful custodian ever since. A visit to the East Neuk of Fife is incomplete without a walk in the aromatic gardens, then a climb up winding stairs to the restored rooms of this family castle.

In the studio at Kellie Castle, a version in plaster of the massive granite statue Our Lady of the Isles, sculpted by Hew Lorimer (1907-93), second son of the architect Sir Robert Lorimer, and an artist whose profound religious convictions found expression in his work. Completed in 1958, Our Lady of the Isles is sited at Rueval on South Uist and has become part of the Hebridean landscape, like the Celtic crosses on Iona.

(Opposite): It has been argued that because of its long period of dereliction, Kellie Castle escaped the Victorian mania for adding extensions to historic buildings, thereby creating architectural imbalance. And even when Professor James Lorimer became the long-term tenant, he did not have the money – or the inclination - to make major alterations or additions. His son Robert respected the original structure in his restoration work, which is why Kellie has been hailed as a 'dramatic poem in stone.'

Is it possible that the barrow of bricks in the nursery at Kellie Castle once belonged to Robert Lorimer, budding architect?